Tiny Time Big Results
4 Principles to Run Your Profitable 20 Hour Week Business

Workbook

Yasmin Vorajee

Copyright

© 2022 Yasmin Vorajee

All rights reserved. This book or any portion thereof may not be reproduced or used in any manner whatsoever without the express written permission of the publisher except for the use of brief quotations in a book review.

The information contained within this Book is strictly for educational purposes. If you wish to apply ideas contained in this Book, you are taking full responsibility for your actions.

The author has made every effort to ensure the accuracy of the information within this book was correct at time of publication. The author does not assume and hereby disclaims any liability to any party for any loss, damage, or disruption caused by errors or omissions, whether such errors or omissions result from accident, negligence, or any other cause.

Published by Stardust Publishing House

Print ISBN: 978-1-9164761-2-7

Front Cover Design: Stardust Publishing House

Book Interior: Stardust Publishing House

For print or media interviews, please contact support@yasminvorajee.com

Visit the website: www.yasminvorajee.com

To get the most out of this book and the Tiny Time community, join the **Tiny Time Book Club** and get instant access to a monthly coaching call and additional resources. Join here www.yasminvorajee.com/jointtbookclub

Table of Contents

Welcome to the Tiny Time Big Results Workbook! 1
The 5 Big QUESTIONS 2
The Purpose Principle 4
    How to Find Your Business Sweet Spot 5
    Who Do You Want To Serve? 9
    Your Big Picture 10
The Profit Principle 12
    Create Your Signature Program. 13
    Your Marketing 15
    Sales and Selling 19
    Client Delight 22
The Productivity Principle 24
    Declutter Your Surroundings. 24
    Managing Your Time & Energy 25
    Standard Operating Procedures 27
    Your To-Do List 28
The Play Principle 31
    The Inner Work 31
    How Do You Raise Your Vibe? 32
    Vision Board 33
    The Outer Work 34
Roadblocks 36
What Is Your Next Step? 37
About Yasmin 39
    Connect with Yasmin 40

WELCOME TO THE TINY TIME BIG RESULTS WORKBOOK!

Hi lovely,

I'm delighted to welcome you to the workbook that is going to power your 20 hour week business!

This workbook is the companion workbook for the #1 bestselling and award winning book, **Tiny Time Big Results** (*if you haven't got it yet, you can get it here www.yasminvorajee.com/book*) and I've designed it so you can actively participate in the process of designing your 20 hour week business...and make it happen!

This is not about being passive, I want you to take action!

Even if you're nowhere near enjoying a profitable 20 hour week business, wouldn't it be amazing if you could reduce your working time by a quarter, a third or even a half without compromising your income and impact? That's what Tiny Time Big Results is all about!

The workbook is for you to create massive clarity, grab yourself a cuppa and give yourself at least an hour to look at your business with a fresh pair of eyes! The questions in the workbook are your prompts for journaling. As an over-thinker myself, I would encourage to *try* not to overthink your answers and let your inner wisdom bring up the answers for you.

Remember, you're a coffee pot....allow yourself to percolate!

So without further ado, let's dive in!

THE 5 BIG QUESTIONS

When you start a journey, you need to know where you are right now in order to chart your travels. This activity is designed to help you take stock of where you are right now.

Rate yourself on a scale of 1-10 for each of the 5 statements,

(1 being not at all, 10 is absolutely!)

1.	My business has a specific and targeted marketing message	/10
2.	My business has a deliberate and strategic marketing strategy that works.	/10
3.	I have a proven way to convert prospects into paying clients.	/10
4.	I have leveraged products, programs and services where I don't trade time for money.	/10
5.	I am focused, efficient and effective with managing your time and energy.	/10

If you have rated less than 8/10 on these 5 statements, what does this tell you?

THE PURPOSE PRINCIPLE

The Purpose Principle is about having:

- A clear purpose for your business
- A compelling vision of what you want to be known for
- A business that plays to your sweet spot of experience, knowledge and expertise
- A magnetic big picture
- A strong statement that outlines **what** you do and **who** you do it for

What is your WHY? Why do you do what you do?

How to Find Your Business Sweet Spot

Step 1 — GOOD AT

You have talents, skills, expertise and experience. Think about your whole career — everything you have done that has brought you to this point.

List out all the jobs you've ever had, starting from your Saturday job in the local supermarket. (*I used to love working on the cash registers!*) Keep going until you have exhausted your memory.

Think about all the experience you have gained, the skills you have learnt, the knowledge you have acquired.

Step 2 — PASSIONATE ABOUT

What are you passionate about? What are you always talking about? What does that little whisper in your heart say to you? What do you think is your 'calling'? Why are you here?

Step 3 — IS THIS REALLY NEEDED?

Are people looking for this solution? Are they googling it? How can you find out? Have you validated your idea?

Step 4: WILL PEOPLE PAY?

If the market you serve is not willing to pay, you will always struggle. Your business will not build traction, nor will it gain momentum. The balance is achieved by working with a group of people you are drawn to work with and who are willing and able to pay.

Who Do You Want To Serve?

Key questions to ask to identify your ideal client:

- What problem do I solve for them?
- Who do I love working with?
- Who can I get a result for fast?
- Does this group know they have a problem?
- Are they looking for a solution?
- Are they willing to pay?
- What is different about this group than others?
- What are their aspirations and fears?
- Why would they gravitate to me and not someone else?

Your Big Picture

Here are some questions to help you create your exciting big picture:

How many hours do you want to work?	
How much money do you want to make?	
How do you want to work with your clients?	
How many weeks a year do you want to work?	

How many holidays will you take off?	
Do you want to have a team?	
Will you have premises?	

THE PROFIT PRINCIPLE

What is your marketing message?

Here's a handy format for you to formulate your statement:

I help

....
(INSERT IDEAL CLIENT)

to ....
(SOLVE THEIR PROBLEM)

so they can ....
(THE RESULT/OUTCOME)

Create Your Signature Program.

There are five steps to create your program:

1. **Promise**: What is the end result that someone will achieve as a result of working with you? What do you promise them?	
2. **Process:** What's the process you take them through to achieve the transformation?	

3. **Package:** How will you package it?	
4. **Price:** How will you price it?	
5. **Leverage:** What streams of income will you create?	

Your Marketing

Which marketing methods will you use/ continue to use/ stop using?

What is/ will be your lead magnet?

What is your short term nurture sequence?

How will you nurture your prospects in the long term?

Sales and Selling

What are your numbers?

What is your pre-selling strategy?

What is your follow up sequence?

Client Delight

How do you on-board and delight your clients and customers and affirm they have made the right decision?

What legal protections do you have in place currently to protect you and your clients and customers?

THE PRODUCTIVITY PRINCIPLE

Declutter Your Surroundings.

Start off with decluttering your space for just 10 minutes each day and you will soon see how powerful decluttering can be for you to clear your mind, body, spirit and energy.

Suggested physical areas to declutter:
- Your desk
- Filing
- Purse/ wallet

Suggested mental areas to declutter:
- Goals and visions – it never hurts to revisit these to make sure they serve you!
- What you think you *should* be doing in business
- Your money fears and blocks

Suggested emotional areas to declutter:
- Comparison-it is – it truly is the thief of joy (*Roosevelt*) so let it go. The only person you can compare yourself to is the person you were yesterday!
- Shame about your business
- Guilt - about anything and everything! It doesn't serve you so let it go!

What will you declutter today?

_____

_____

_____

_____

Managing Your Time & Energy

Determine your work hours/ office hours

What are your goals for the next 90 days? Break them down into months, weeks and days

Standard Operating Procedures

Begin to document your processes so you can create standard operating procedures to make life easier for yourself and when you begin to outsource, delegating will be a lot less stressful.

You just need 3 simple headings to get started:

- PROJECT (*what does this activity relate to?*)
- ACTION (*this is where you need to get detailed and granular*)
- WHO'S RESPONSIBLE

PROJECT	ACTION	WHO'S RESPONSIBLE
e.g. weekly marketing content	*In this section, you document each step of how you create, produce and share your weekly content* *List as 1, 2, 3...*	*Me and VA*

Your To-Do List

What are you going to...?

DO	DITCH	DELEGATE

What can you start to outsource?

What is your PLAN – DO – REVIEW routine?

_____
_____
_____
_____
_____
_____
_____

How will you hold yourself accountable?

_____
_____
_____
_____
_____
_____
_____
_____
_____
_____

THE PLAY PRINCIPLE

The Inner Work

Trust & Value Yourself:

Make a list of all the clients you have helped and write down the result you helped them create. Stack them high. Think of every single client you've ever worked with — free or paid — and write it all down. Look at the testimonials you have. And if you don't have testimonials, I would encourage doing a number of free sessions and asking for a testimonial in return, so others can see the transformation you create.

How Do You Raise Your Vibe?

If you want to achieve a goal, your energy needs to resonate at the same frequency as your goal.

Set yourself a goal (for this example, let's choose a money goal)

Making 5k a month

In your journal, ask yourself what making 5k would do for you. What would it allow you to do? How would you feel when you made 5k? Describe it in as much detail as possible, then sit in the energy of already achieving it. Scan your body to see how it feels in your toes, your fingers, your spine, your head, your chest and all over your body.

Take four deep breaths to breathe the outcome in.

List out all the ways you raise your vibration.....in other words, what makes you feel good?!

Mine include dancing, listening to music, cooking, jumping on the trampoline, tickling my babies, doing yoga and read uplifting books.

_____

_____

_____

_____

Vision Board

Take some time to create your vision board.

Here's how to get started. Take 15 minutes to jot down up to 10 things you want to make real in the next three years. It could be a dream home, a trip to Hawaii, a sleek office space, your published book or an incredible family holiday in Australia.

Get some magazines and cut out pictures or words that represent what you want in life and business. It could be cars, homes, gorgeous clients or fab food — pick what inspires you, motivates you and gets your heart racing!

Put things on your vision board that include your future aspirations AS WELL as what you have already achieved (*this amps up the high vibe feeling!*)

The Outer Work

What's your morning routine? How do you set yourself up to win? (*I have a nifty checklist that will help you do this in just 7 minutes - you can grab it for free here www.yasminvorajee.com/daily-checklist*)

When is your digital detox day? When do you switch off?

What does 'play' look like for you? How can you incorporate more play in your days?

ROADBLOCKS

What could stop you in your tiny time journey? How can you overcome them?

WHAT IS YOUR NEXT STEP?

Congratulations on completing the Tiny Time Big Results workbook!

You've shown you're truly committed to creating a profitable business in 20 hours a week or less.

Every tiny action you take creates a ripple effect and that is powerful so please don't ever underestimate this!

It's always my intention to give you as much value as possible.

But I know that information is one thing, implementation is another.

It can be so easy to get caught up in everyday life and not focus on what really makes your business work which is why I have created my courses and programs for you!

Through my courses, you can have your

- ✓ Compelling leveraged offers designed and ready!
- ✓ Irresistible Lead Magnet created and live
- ✓ Authentic short term nurture sequence written/recorded and automated so people can fall in love with you and your work
- ✓ Long term nurture plan created for the next 6 months – no more 'spray and pray'!
- ✓ Appointment diary ready to be filled with qualified leads!
- ✓ Sales process pinned down and ready to go so you can raise the roof on your conversion rate!

This **doesn't** happen by accident, these are deliberate actions you take that ensure you attract clients and income consistently.

My courses and programs are designed to help you do this, through **projects and guided implementation** so you are taking action every step of the way!

Every tiny action counts!

If you would like to know more about my courses and programs, you can DM me on Instagram to get more info (*@yasvorajee*) and you can also check out my website www.yasminvorajee.com

If you have any questions about this workbook or Tiny Time, don't forget to connect with me on my website or DM me on social media.

And if you prefer email, you can message me at support@yasminvorajee.com

All my best!

ABOUT YASMIN

Yasmin Vorajee is the creator of Tiny Time Big Results where she teaches service business owners how to run a profitable business in 20 hours a week or less.

A former Vice President of Leadership Development, Yasmin specialises in business and marketing strategy and runs her thriving business from her home in rural Ireland where she lives with her husband and their 3 young children.

Yasmin is from the UK and has lived in Ireland for the last 21 years. She is passionate about helping people create fulfilment in their work and financial abundance so families can spend more time together, connect deeply and enjoy life fully.

Yasmin has featured in local, national and international media including the Irish Times, the Irish Independent, Dublin City FM, The Huffington Post, Tatler Magazine, Tesco Magazine, Evoke and the Sunday Independent.

Yasmin helps small business owners to

- **Nail** your marketing **message** so it's **clear, compelling and magnetic!**
- **Design products and programs** that make it easy for you to be profitable in 20 hours a week (*or less*)
- **Create** and **implement** an **authentic** and **powerful marketing strategy**
- **Manage your energy, not time** and get the right things done (*the things that actually make a difference!*). No more being **glued to your phone** or laptop all the time!

On a personal note, Yasmin loves food and you'll find her either making it, eating it or thinking about it!

Connect with Yasmin

- Join the Tiny Time Book Club: www.yasminvorajee.com/jointtbookclub/
- Join the free Tiny Time Tribe Facebook Group: www.facebook.com/groups/tinytimetribe
- Take 30 seconds and 'Like' Tiny Time Big Results on Facebook: www.facebook.com/tinytimebigresultswithYasminVorajee
- Email Yasmin at support@yasminvorajee.com
- Follow Yasmin on Twitter @tinytimewithyas
- Connect with Yasmin on Linkedin
- Follow Yasmin on Instagram @yasvorajee
- For media, print or podcast interview, please contact support@yasminvorajee.com

www.ingramcontent.com/pod-product-compliance
Lightning Source LLC
Chambersburg PA
CBHW061347040426
42444CB00011B/3123